Literacy Centers in Photographs

by Nikki Campo-Stallone

New York • Toronto • London • Auckland • Sydney
New Delhi • Mexico City • Hong Kong • Buenos Aires

Teaching Resources

Dedication

I dedicate this book to my wonderful family. Thank you to my parents Nicholas and Marilyn Campo. They have guided and encouraged me to become the teacher I am today. To my sister, Kristy, who has always been a source of strength in my life. Finally, to my loving husband, Matt, who has supported me in this journey from start to finish. I love and thank you all!

Acknowledgments

I would like to thank the William Floyd School District for supporting me in this project. I would also like to acknowledge the many students who have been a part of my life as a teacher. You continue to be my inspiration.

Cover design by Brian LaRossa
Interior design by Grafica Inc.
Cover and interior photographs by Brian LaRossa, Jaime Lucero, and Nikki Campo-Stallone
ISBN-13 978-0-545-00798-6
ISBN-10 0-545-00798-4

Contents

Introduction

When I first imagined having a classroom of my own, I knew that I wanted to create a space in which children would learn to work together, share materials, and have many opportunities to hold rich conversations that would further their learning. I also wanted a classroom that fostered independence. Creating and using literacy centers supports my vision of this kind of classroom.

In this book, I've included photographs to show how I set up each of the centers in my classroom, as well as how I introduce them to my students. You'll also find photographs that help you see the routines and procedures I use to support children's independent use of the centers. My hope is that this book will help you get started with literacy centers—and help your students be successful learners.

Chapter 1

Organizing Your Classroom for Centers

Center time takes place in my classroom at the same time I'm working with guided reading groups. Groups of students move from center to center, while I read with a group. It takes several weeks to establish the routines necessary for students to move among centers independently. In this chapter, I'll show you how I organize my classroom so that not only do literacy centers run smoothly, but my classroom becomes a true community where children develop the skills they need to become independent learners.

Classroom Layout

Here's a diagram that shows the layout of my classroom at the start of the school year. I have five student tables, and each one seats four to six children. Each child has an assigned seat at one of the tables. I tape a laminated label with the child's name on it so that it is clear who sits where. I also assign a color to each table by hanging a large sign in that color above the table. Then, I color code materials and supplies for that table using the same color. This makes it easier for children to find and return the supplies and materials.

At center time, four student tables become centers. In addition to the table centers, six other centers are set up in different areas of the classroom. During center time, children leave their assigned seats and move from center to center. As you'll read in Chapter 5, I introduce the centers gradually during the first six to eight weeks of school. Until children know the center routines, I don't begin meeting with groups for guided reading. I wait until I know that children can stay focused and on task as they work in centers.

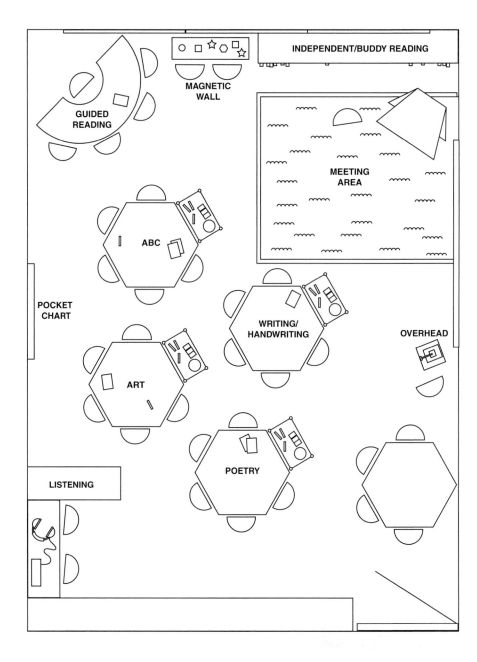

Classroom Supplies

One way to create a community of learners in the classroom is by having community supplies. During the summer, I send a note home to parents about supplies. I list the supplies each student will need, but I also explain that these supplies will be shared among all the students in the class. I ask parents to help foster this sharing by not labeling supplies with their child's name. (See Appendix B for a sample letter.)

On the first day of school, I collect all of the supplies that children have brought in. I store some of them so I can replenish supplies later in the year. I sort the rest into separate bins and place the bins on each student table.

> **TIP**
> Label each bin clearly with words and pictures.

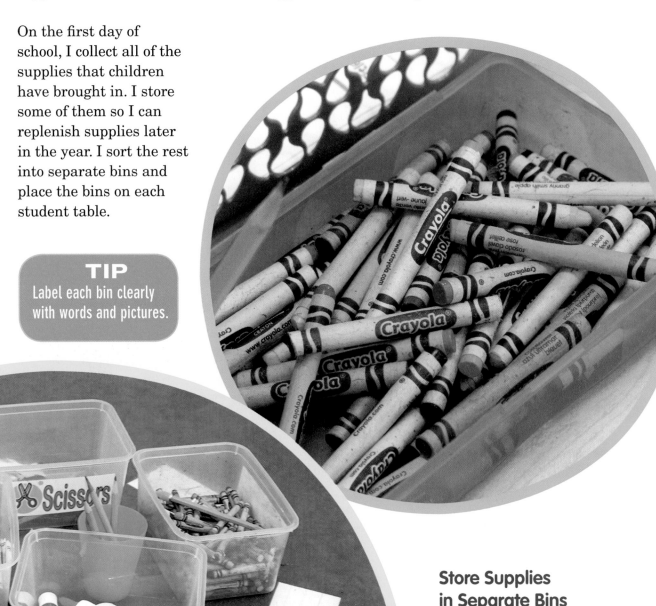

Store Supplies in Separate Bins

I find that keeping the supplies in separate bins gives children the best access to them. If one student is using the crayon bin, another can use the marker bin.

Supplies Shelf

I also place a shelf at each table. Any student folders, materials, notebooks, and so on are placed on the bottom two shelves. Center supplies are placed on the top shelf. This keeps supplies readily available, helps to limit how often students need to move around the classroom, and makes transitions between activities quicker and easier.

Writing Folder Crates

At each table I keep a crate that holds writing workshop folders. The crate is labeled with the table color. Each folder is clearly labeled with the writing workshop icon and each child's name. (See Appendix A for center icons.)

Notebook Baskets

At each table there are baskets to house each type of notebook that the children use. The notebooks are easy to access and distribute when needed.

Storytelling Baskets

At the beginning of the school year, I have children create storytelling bags at home. These bags house photos or items that represent memories. The items help to spark writing ideas. The children refill the bags every trimester. (See Appendix C for a sample letter to send home.)

Table Jobs

I find it helpful for children at each table to have clearly defined jobs. Having jobs fosters a sense of responsibility. The jobs rotate weekly so that every child has the opportunity to try each one. I attach the laminated list of jobs to the bottom of the colored sign hanging above the table and use clothespins with children's names to indicate job assignments.

TABLE JOBS

 Writing Folders — Christian

 ABC Notebooks — Skyler

12 3 Math Notebooks — Felicity

 Bucket Organizer — Antonio

Writing Folders Job

This child passes out and collects the writing folders for his or her table during writing workshop.

Word Study Notebooks Job

This child passes out and collects the word study notebooks for his or her table when needed.

Math Notebooks Job

This child passes out and collects the math notebooks for his or her table when needed.

Bucket Organizer Job

This child keeps the supply buckets neat and organized. The student also checks to make sure the caps are on the markers and glue.

Table Centers

During center time, each student table in my classroom becomes a different center.

Center Materials

Any supplies needed for participation in a center are stored on the shelf next to that table along with students' other supplies. This ensures easy access to these necessary materials.

Label Your Table Centers

To show children what center the table is, I attach a laminated icon to the bottom of the hanging colored sign, along with the laminated list of jobs associated with that table. (See Appendix A for center icons.)

Literacy Center Board

As I work with a guided reading group, I want all the other children in my class to be learning at centers—and to move from center to center independently. To make sure this happens, I developed what I call our "literacy center board." At the top of the board, there is a card with a list of children's names—for my class, I have five cards, with the names of four to six children on each one. These cards tell children who is in each group. Beneath each list, place four cards, each with a center icon on it. This makes it very easy for each child to figure out independently which center he or she should be working at, and when.

Here are some possibilities for creating a literacy centers board.

A magnetic blackboard

You can adhere magnets to the backs of your icon cards and display them on the blackboard.

A pocket chart

A presentation board

If you use a presentation board, you can take it out during center time and put it away when done.

A felt board

Velcro on the back of each icon allows it to stick to the board.

Having clear rules and routines for your centers will make them run smoothly. In the next chapter, we'll look at some of the center routines I've found to be effective in my classroom.

Chapter 2

Putting Center Routines in Place

One of the most crucial components of a successful literacy center experience is having effective routines. It's important to dedicate time to teaching and practicing these routines with children. Children respond well to structure and clear expectations. In this chapter, we'll look at some of the general center rules and routines I establish with children. In chapters 3 and 4, we'll take a closer look at the specific rules and routines for each center.

Noise Level

It is important to be clear with children about your expectations regarding noise levels in the classroom. One of the first routines I introduce to students involves helping them develop an understanding of "whisper work voices." Some centers require mostly silence, while others require cooperative learning that may include some conversation. Children need to be aware of the volume of their voice so that other students in the class can concentrate and focus. I find it important to model what a whisper work voice sounds like and have children practice speaking in a whisper work voice to ensure their understanding.

Although most center activities require children to speak in whisper work voices most of the time, there may be times when your expectations change. For example, during an independent reading activity, you may want your room to be silent. When children are sharing something they've written, you may want them to use a talking voice. Regardless of the activity, when children are made aware of your expectations they are more likely to meet them.

Noise Level Stoplight

A noise level stoplight is one way for children to visualize your expectations. When I place the magnet on red, children know that it is a no-talking time. If I place the magnet on yellow, children recognize that it is okay to use a whisper work voice. When the magnet is on green, children understand that they may use a talking voice.

Bathroom Use Rules

Another important routine I try to put in place early in the school year is how I want children to make me aware of their need to use the bathroom. I clearly explain the steps I want them to follow: 1) find a buddy, 2) get the bathroom pass, and 3) show me the pass. I explain that if I am working with a guided reading group, they need to make sure that I acknowledge them with a nod before they leave the classroom. This procedure allows children to communicate their needs to me without interrupting others' work.

Asking Questions

During center time, children may have questions related to a center activity. In order to minimize interruptions, I encourage children to "ask three times before you ask me." This means that children need to ask three classmates before coming to me. Having this routine in place allows children to use one another as a resource. Of course, emergencies are always the exception to this rule!

Calling Reading Groups

As children are working independently at centers, I'm working with one group, doing guided reading. Since guided reading groups are meant to be flexible, student membership in these groups changes as children's needs change. Therefore, the children you call to the reading table may be different from week to week. To get the attention of my class in a way that is not too intrusive, I ring a soft bell. The children know that when they hear the bell, they need to put their eyes on me. I then hold up a reading group calling card that lists the names of children who will be meeting with me. (See Appendix D for copies of guided reading group calling cards.) If students see their name, they need to clean up their work and join me at the table. If they do not see their name, they continue with their work. I have discovered that if I call children in the least intrusive way possible, they are more likely to continue their work at an appropriate voice level.

(See Appendix D for copies of guided reading group calling cards.)

TIPS

Laminate each of your guided reading group calling cards. Then use a dry-erase marker to write the names of the children in that group. This enables you to erase and easily change the names as your groups change throughout the year.

Rain Stick

While students are working at their centers, they may need a gentle reminder to keep their voice level at a whisper. I remind them by using a rain stick. It has a very soft "shushing" sound that helps children stay on task.

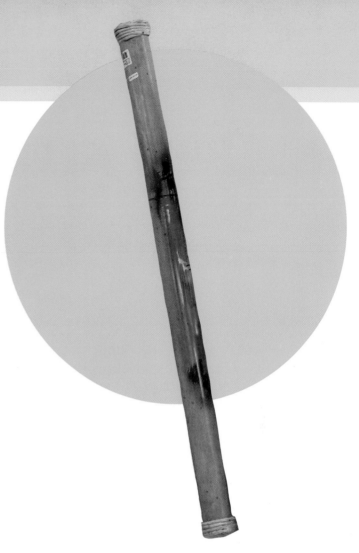

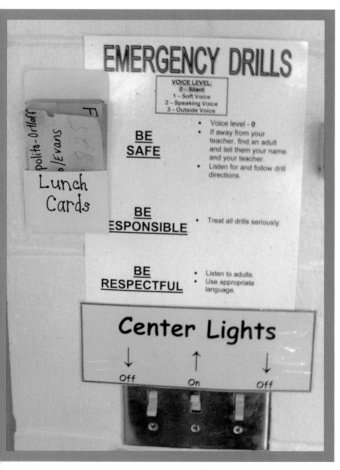

Center Lights

In my classroom, I have three light switches, each one controlling a different set of lights. I always ask a child turn off two of the three light switches right before center time. The first time I do this, I mention that dim lighting creates a soothing atmosphere. This soothing atmosphere gives children another visual reminder of the voice level they should be using.

In Chapter 3, we'll look at how each of the literacy centers is organized.

Chapter 3

Taking a Closer Look at the Centers

When organizing centers for student use, I try to think carefully about what students need in order to be independent and successful. For example, I try to store materials so that they can be easily accessed, and I provide resources that will support children as they work in a center. In this chapter, I am going to take you through each of the different centers in my classroom so that you can see the organizational structures I've put in place to foster student independence.

Buddy Reading

A t the buddy reading center, children work in pairs, taking turns reading a book to each other.

Organization and Routines

Choosing Buddies

In the first row on my literacy center board (see pages 16-17), I place a card that lists the names of the children who will visit the center that day. (In kindergarten, I also include photos of students.) I list the names in a way that makes it clear who the pairs are. I find that assigning buddies, rather than letting children choose their own partners, alleviates potential problems. I usually change the buddy pairs once a month so that children have the opportunity to work with many different buddies throughout the course of the school year.

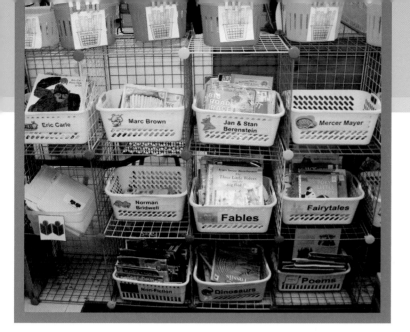

Buddy Reading Library

This center requires an area for storing and organizing appropriate books as well as children's buddy reading folders. I organize the books in my buddy reading library in baskets on shelves. I often separate them by theme, genre, or author.

Buddy Reading Library Book Baskets

Be sure to clearly label the baskets of books in your buddy reading library. I use icons to represent the types of books in each basket. I also print the icons onto stickers and affix them to the books. This helps students return the books to the appropriate basket, keeping the library organized.

Buddy Reading Rules

In order for my students to have a good understanding of what is expected during buddy reading time, we brainstorm rules for this center, using interactive writing.

TIP

I always invite children to help create the rules for all our centers. When students are involved in creating the rules, they become much more invested in the routines—and the centers run more smoothly.

Logging in Buddy Reading Books

In order for students to be accountable at this center, I ask them to record the title and author of each book they are reading. Each student is given a buddy reading folder with the buddy reading icon on the cover, his or her name on the tab, and a reading record sheet stapled inside. (See Appendix E.) Each time a student completes a sheet, I staple a new one on top of it. By the end of the year, students have a clear record of the books they have read during buddy reading. When students are ready to respond to their books independently, I have them complete a reading response activity, and then file it in on the other side of the file folder.

Buddy Reading Record Sheet

Date .... Buddy ....

Title ....

Author ....

Date .... Buddy ....

Title ....

Author ....

Housing Buddy Reading Folders

It is important that your students' buddy reading folders be easy to access. I clearly label this basket and store it within the buddy reading library.

Buddy Reading in Motion

Here's how buddy reading works. Buddies visit the buddy reading library to select a book. Both children select a book so that they will share two stories. Since each child is given the opportunity to choose a book, there are no arguments about who will pick a book.

Once each child has selected a book, the pair looks for a quiet place to read together. I model for them how to pick a spot to read. They should look for a space that does not have a lot of other children around. It should be a quiet area with minimal distractions.

Once they have found a quiet place to read, students can work together to decide which book they plan to read first. I expect children to sit in a way that is conducive to sharing their books. For instance, the children in the photo are sitting side by side and holding the book between them.

Early in the year, children may not be independent readers yet. During buddy reading, I have children work together to tell the story through the pictures in the book if the words are too difficult. This gives them a sense of confidence and the opportunity to independently enjoy challenging picture books. This process also helps build the students' sense of story—and develop their love of books.

Once the buddies have completed both books, I have them write the title and author of the books they have read in their buddy reading folder.

Independent Reading

G iving children time to read independently is an important part of my literacy program. My independent reading center includes lots of books at a range of reading levels.

Organization and Routines

Independent Reading Library

In order to monitor children's independent reading, I find it helpful to level the books in my library. I want children to have the opportunity to select a book that is just right for them, so I put books at a range of several levels within a basket, giving children the chance to make an appropriate choice. For instance, I place books at guided reading levels A–E in red bins, levels F–I in orange bins, levels J–L in yellow bins, and levels M–N in green bins. I may also choose not to put bins out if I do not currently have children reading at those levels.

1.	Isabella	●	
2.	Skyler	●●	
3.	Daniel	●●	
4.	Christian	●●	
5.	Dylan	●	
6.	Antonio	●●	
7.	Ramona	●●	
8.	Ashley	●●	
9.	Jazmyn	●	
10.	Vinny	●	
11.	Julia	●●	
12.	Zara	●●	
13.	Serena	●●	
14.	Felicity	●●	
15.	Michelle	●●	
16.	Jonathan	●●	
17.	Robert	●●	
18.	Traivon	●●	
19.	Matthew	●	
20.	Dabney	●●	
21.	Sereyna	●●	
22.	Raegan	●●	
23.	Faith	●	
24.	Jimmy	●●	

Guiding Your Students

Students need a way to know which basket has an appropriate range of books for them to read. To help them with this, I post a class list in a clear plastic photograph frame. Next to each child's name, I color in a dot that represents the basket that is appropriate for them. This list is flexible, of course, changing as the year progresses.

A Closer Look at the Independent Reading Chart

This row helps Ramona know which bin includes appropriate books for independent reading. By looking at the chart, she will be guided to either the orange or yellow bin to select books to read.

Housing Independent Reading Folders

Students will need to know where to find their independent reading folders in order to make this center run smoothly. I keep the independent reading basket above the independent reading library, next to the class list that notes which basket they should select books from.

Logging in Independent Reading Books

As I did with the buddy reading center, I want students to be accountable for completing their reading. Each student has an independent reading folder that I create out of a pocket file folder. In the folder, I include a sheet for recording the titles and authors of the books he or she reads. (See Appendix F.) I put the independent reading icon on the cover, along with the child's name on the tab, and inside I staple the log sheet. Each time students complete a sheet, I staple a new one on top of it. This way, they have a clear record of the books they have read independently throughout the year—and having a list of all the wonderful books they've read is a source of pride for students! On the other side of the file folder, students can store any reading response papers they complete when they're ready to do this kind of work independently.

Independent Reading in Motion

During independent reading, the first thing students need to know is how to check the independent reading chart to see which bin is appropriate for them. Show them how to find their name and how to match the color of the sticker to the sticker on the appropriate basket.

Next, have your students look through the appropriate baskets in order to select a book that is just right for them to read on their own.

Once a student has selected a book to read independently, he or she should look for a place to read. I encourage students to look for places that are quiet and away from distraction so they can concentrate on their reading.

Poetry

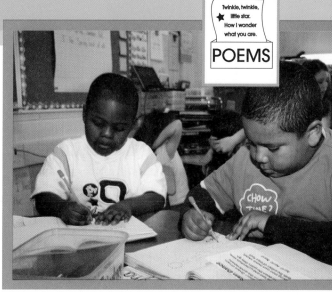

Poetry, with its rhymes and rhythms, is a wonderful way to get children exploring language. At this center, children have a chance to respond to poems we have read during shared reading, and to practice reading the poems on their own.

Organization and Routines

Designate a Table

I set up my poetry center at one of the student tables. Children need to use scissors, pencils, and crayons at this center, so having supplies already available is very helpful. I also place two baskets on the shelf at this table—one for copies of the poem that children will work on, and the other for children's poetry notebooks.

Choosing Poems for the Centers

The poems I place in the poetry center are ones I have previously introduced during shared reading. I find that it's important for children to have a clear working knowledge of the poem and to be able to read it independently before it is placed in a center. In addition to the copies I have for students, I hang an enlarged version of the poem near the center for children to refer to and read.

Poetry Notebook

Each child has a poetry notebook. These notebooks are stored on the shelf next to the poetry center table. This gives students easy access to their notebooks during center time.

On the cover of the poetry notebook, I include the student's name and a label to make the notebook easy to locate.

Copies of the Poems

Children paste a copy of the week's poem into their notebooks. Be sure the copies of the poem you provide are small enough to fit in children's notebooks. After pasting the poem in their notebooks, children create an illustration that reflects the content of the poem. When they are ready, you can ask them to respond to the poem in writing to show that they have understood it.

Poetry Center Rules

Again, work with students to create rules for the poetry center. Once you have created these rules, post them near the center so that children can use them as a reference. Be sure to use simple language and include pictures whenever possible.

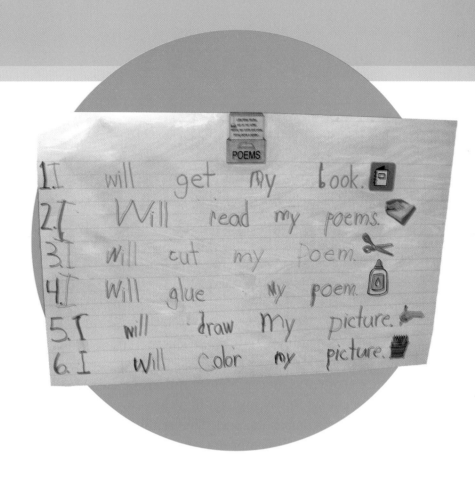

Poetry Center in Motion

Children begin by cutting out the poem from the sheet I've provided. I always include a box around the poem so children have lines they can cut along. Cutting out the poem also gives them an opportunity to practice fine-motor skills.

Next, they glue the poem into their notebooks. They should glue the poem onto one left page of a two-page spread. On the opposite page, children can illustrate and respond to the poem. Illustrating the poem enhances children's comprehension of it, while helping them develop their drawing skills. I have them draw in pencil first, and then color the illustration.

Once students can confidently illustrate their poems, I invite them to respond to the poems in writing. As the year progresses, I increase the difficulty of the types of responses I expect. This scaffolds their learning and both deepens and strengthens their comprehension of poetry.

Pocket Chart

The pocket chart center can be used for a variety of activities. Sometimes I use it as another way to support children with a word study lesson. I also use it with poetry. On sentence strips I write words or phrases from a poem we've read in shared reading. Students can then manipulate and read the words in poems, using the pocket chart. Also, once a poem has rotated through the poetry center, I may move it to the poetry pocket chart.

Organization and Routines

Designate an Area

For the pocket chart center, choose an area in your room where you can hang a pocket chart that students can use daily. A pocket chart stand might work, or you can try to find a way to adhere the chart to a wall. The pocket chart shown in the photograph is drilled into the concrete wall in my classroom, but I have also stapled the pocket chart to the wall when my classroom didn't have concrete walls. Be sure that the pocket chart is at eye level and can be reached by all students. Also keep in mind that the center area needs to have enough open floor space for children to be able to spread out the sentence strips in order to piece the poem together.

Storing the Letter Cards and Word or Sentence Strips

I have found that the best way to store the materials students will use in the pocket chart is in a manila envelope. I cut off the top of the envelope, punch holes in the corners, and use yarn or string to hang it nearby. You can also hang the envelope on a hook, a thumbtack, or a hat rack. When using the center for word study activities, you can write the directions for the activity on the front of the envelope. If students are working with poetry at the center, print a copy of the poem on the outside of the envelope. This will give your students the opportunity to self-check their work and correct any mistakes that they have made.

Pocket Chart Rules

With your students, write rules for your pocket chart center during shared or interactive writing. Make sure that the language is simple, and have children reread the rules each time they go to the center. You may need to change the rules depending upon what kind of activity the children are using the pocket chart for. The rules in this photo are for organizing word strips in a poem, and then finding consonant blends in the poem.

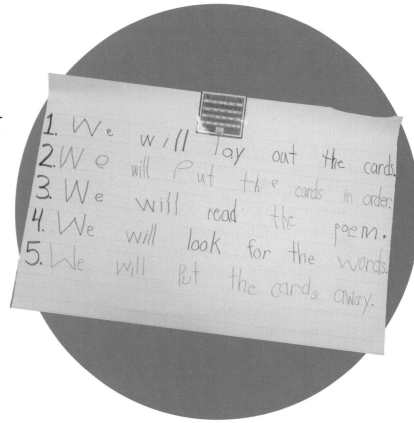

Pocket Chart Center in Motion

These photos show children using the pocket chart to figure out the order of words in a poem. I always encourage children to build the poem from left to right to develop reading skills. I hang the enlarged copy of the poem nearby to assist them. This also gives them another way to check their work.

Once the poem has been completed in the pocket chart, have the children read it together several times. You can also ask children to highlight words that go along with the word principle you are working on. For instance, these students are using a fly swatter with a hole cut out of it and a pointer to locate consonant blends in the poem.

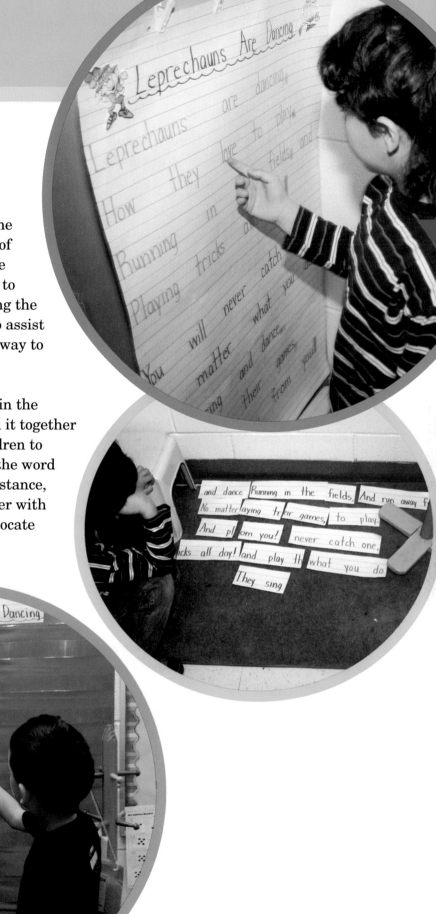

Listening

At this center, children can listen to books on tape as they follow along in the text.

Organization and Routines

Materials

You will need a tape player, books, and tapes on which you've recorded the books. You might also want to have headphones. It's important to have several copies of each book at the center, so that each student can follow along in his or her own book.

If your children are ready to write in response to their listening, provide a basket in which to store the response sheets. Also provide supplies such as pens, pencils, markers, and crayons

Designate a Space

I set up my listening center at a table in a corner area, so that any sound issues are minimized.

Listening Center Response

You can have your students complete a response after listening to the story. In the early literacy stages, I ask children just to illustrate their favorite part of the story. (See Appendix G for a listening center early response sheet.) As the students become more-independent writers, I invite them to write in response to the stories that they read. (See Appendix H for a listening center written response sheet.)

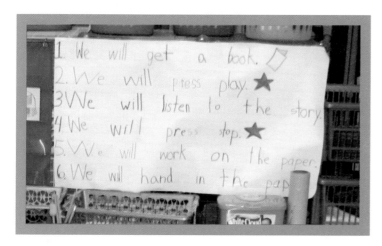

Create Listening Center Rules

You can work with your students to create rules or steps to follow when at the listening center. Be sure to keep the language simple and post the rules nearby. Use picture symbols whenever possible.

TIP
If you decide not to have children use headphones, be sure that you record your tapes at a volume that students at the center can hear, but that won't disrupt children at other centers.

Designate Listening Center Jobs

One of the problems that teachers often face at the listening center is that children argue over who will press play, and who will press stop. In order to prevent this, you can designate these roles. Note that I include a green star on the rules chart after step 2, and a red star after step 4. I also post a chart and use clothespins with a red or green star to indicate who has which job. I rotate the jobs each time a group goes to the center.

Post a job reminder To help children be more independent in this center, post a reminder of what the green star and the red star mean.

Label the tape recorder I put the same green star on the play button and the same red star on the stop button.

Listening Center in Motion

At the center, children choose a book and tape. After listening to the book, they complete a response form. When rules and routines are clearly stated and modeled, children know how to use this center appropriately.

ABC

T he ABC center provides a place for children to practice any word study lessons you have previously taught.

Organization and Routines

Designate a Space

This center is most successful when it is set up at a student table, because this gives children a place to write and allows them easy access to table supplies, such as scissors, glue, markers, and crayons.

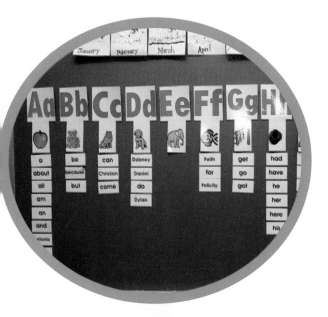

Post an Alphabet Chart

Since children work a great deal with letters and sounds at this center, I like to post an alphabet chart near the table for them to use as a reference.

Storage of Center Materials

I provide paper for children to write on as well as magnetic letters for children to manipulate as they work. I store these materials in baskets or bins on the shelf near the center.

ABC Center in Motion

The possibilities for ABC center activities are endless! In my classroom, the ABC center changes weekly. I teach a particular word principle for a week, and once students grasp the concept, I know they are ready to practice it independently at the ABC center. It's important for children to have experienced the center activity before I ask them to do it independently.

Word Principle Of The Week!

Some consonant clusters stand for one sound that are different from either of the letters. You can call them consonant digraphs.

sh-	ch-	th-		wh-
she	chip	the	that	where
shout	chop	they		when
shut	chalk	then		what
fish	cheese	this		why
brush	each	there		who

Magnetic Wall

The magnetic wall center is another place where word study concepts are practiced.

Organization and Routines

Designate a Space

Take a look around your classroom to see whether there are any magnetic surfaces. In some classrooms, the heating/cooling unit has a magnetic surface. You can also hang a magnetic white board low to the ground for children to use as a center. You might even be able to square off a section of your blackboard to be used as a magnetic wall center. If you are having trouble finding a space, you can have the children use small magnetic boards on the carpet, giving each child his or her own board to use for the activity.

Storing Materials

Make sure you have all materials nearby. I have a shelf near the center on which I store individual bins, cups of markers, and a paper sorter to hold any papers students need to complete.

Magnetic Wall Center in Motion

At this center, students can practice building the words that they are learning in class. These words might be high-frequency words or words with similar spelling patterns or vowel sounds. Always remind students to build the words from left to right, just as they would when writing.

I keep markers in the colors that match the magnetic letters nearby for any written activities associated with the center. Children love to record their word by using the same colors as the magnetic letters.

Writing

Themed stationery, storytelling bags, and engaging photographs are some of the ways I try to motivate students to write at the writing center.

Organization and Routines

Designate a Space

This center works best when set up at a student table because it gives students full use of the supplies buckets that are already stored there. Students will need to use pencils, markers, crayons, scissors, and glue.

Organize Writing Paper

In order to maximize the use of space, you may want to use paper tray stackers to hold different kinds of writing paper. I keep vertically lined paper, horizontally lined writing paper, and writing stationery. I also have construction paper available for students to create their own books. You can also supply themed stationery. As each season or holiday comes around, change the paper.

Create Writing Center Rules

Work with children to create rules or steps to follow at the writing center. Be sure to keep the language simple and to post the rules so children can easily refer to them.

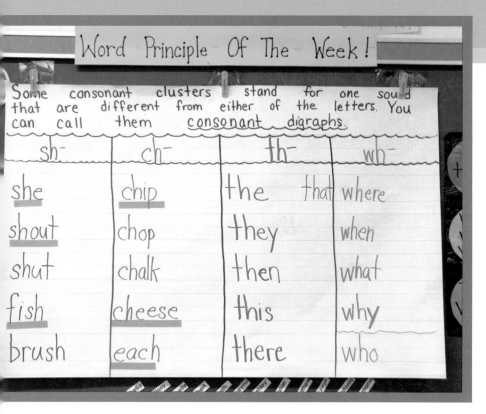

Word Principle Of The Week!

Some consonant clusters stand for one sound that are different from either of the letters. You can call them __consonant digraphs.__

sh-	ch-	th-		wh-
she	chip	the	that	where
shout	chop	they		when
shut	chalk	then		what
fish	cheese	this		why
brush	each	there		who

Provide Resources

Your students may need some resources to support their ability to work independently. For example, you may want to post a copy of an alphabet chart, or you may want to provide a copy of the word principle that you are currently working on. Ready references such as these will encourage your students to practice the lessons that are being taught in the classroom.

A Handwriting Center

In addition to writing, I want my students to work on their handwriting skills. I have them practice letter formation during center time at least once a week. This center works best if set up at a student table.

Writing Center in Motion

At this center, children follow the rules that we created together. To motivate children, I often make use of outdated calendars. The photos from these calendars can spark writing ideas for a creative story. Calendars with different themes and photographs are sure to meet the many interests that many children may have. Most children choose to create their own illustration before they write.

Overhead

C hildren are eager to work at this fun center because they love using the projector.

Organization and Routines

Designate a Space

Find a space in your room that can accommodate your overhead projector and allow it to project against an open surface. If you have a low easel, you can place the overhead projector on the floor and have it project onto the easel. It can also project onto wall space if an easel is not available. Just tape a large piece of blank chart paper to the wall for a clean surface to project on. In order to make the overhead portable, you can place it on a small scooter or a filing cabinet rolling base.

Using the Overhead Projector

In a manila envelope, I store transparencies for children to use with the overhead projector.

Overhead Center in Motion

The overhead projector is a great tool for helping students revisit poems that you have previously shared in class. Each time we complete a poem in class, I copy it onto a transparency and place it in an envelope near the overhead. This gives students a large variety of poems to choose from.

Once students have selected a poem, they place it on the overhead projector and turn it on. Next, students take turns using a pointer to point to each word in the poem as they read it. This is a great activity for building fluency and expression.

At the very bottom of each poem transparency, I write four high-frequency words that I want students to hunt for in the poem. Once they have read the poem several times, their job is to locate and highlight the high-frequency words.

Here a student uses a fly swatter that has a window cut out to assist her in locating the high-frequency words. If the projection is on a white board or chalkboard, you can have students underline or circle the high-frequency words in the poem.

Art

The art center gives your students an opportunity to strengthen their fine-motor skills and develop their illustrating capabilities.

Organization and Routines

Designate a Space

It is best to use one of your student tables for this center because the supplies buckets will be needed.

Supply Shelf

Other center supplies are stored on the top of the shelf nearby. Here I keep a bucket for paper that I want students to use for their artwork. Early in the school year, you may choose to have students focus on the illustrations. (See Appendix I for the early version of the art center sheet.) Later in the school year, you may want to have children add writing to match their illustrations. (See Appendix J for the written art center sheet.)

In another bucket on the supply shelf, I store the directions sheet for the center. Each week, the children learn how to draw a new object by following multi-step directions. I always encourage children to draw with a pencil first in case they make a mistake. Each week, after children have visited the center and completed the illustration, I add the directions to a special "illustration box" in the classroom. Children can then use the directions as resource when they are illustrating something during writing workshop.

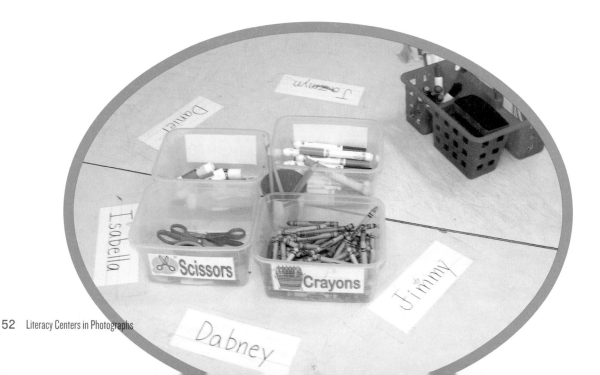

Art Center in Motion

Here students work to follow the multi-step directions to create self-portraits. Once students complete the portrait, they can write about their illustration.

In Chapter 4, we'll take a look at how you can organize students' center work.

Chapter 4

Organizing Students' Center Work

Once you have organized your classroom and set up your centers, you're ready for your students to get to work! As children move through the centers, you'll need to decide how you want to collect the work that they complete. I have developed some clear and simple routines for children to follow so that they can work independently.

Housing Student Work

Finished Work Shelves

One way to organize children's work is to allocate specific storage space on shelves labeled with each center's icon. This will keep work from each center separated, and make it easy for you to look through the work quickly to find some good pieces to share. At the end of each day, you can empty the shelves and review the work students have completed.

Here I have used stacked paper sorters to create a shelving unit. Using the reduce function on a photocopier, I was able to attach small versions of the center icons to each shelf.

Center Folders

After I have checked a student's work, I place it in his or her center folder. On one side of the folder I place finished work, and on the other side any unfinished work. This allows you to house each student's work in one place. Children can revisit the unfinished work on days when they have completed all of that day's center work and still have time left.

You can also choose to have your students use just the center folder and not the shelves. Children can carry their folders from center to center, placing finished work on one side, and any unfinished work on the other. If you plan to have your children do this, be sure to label the two sides of the folder clearly to foster independence.

Sharing Student Work

Star Work Board

In order for children to have clear expectations about their work, it is a good idea to show them what quality work looks like. I created a star work board in my classroom to help children see what my expectations for each center are. Find a bulletin board or an empty space on your wall on which you can display quality completed work. (See Appendix M for star work board icons.) Designate an area on the board for each of your centers that produces something. As you come across quality work for a center, have the child who created it share it. Then discuss with your class what makes it a quality piece. After sharing the piece, post it on the board. Change each example as you change your centers so that the children are exposed to a lot of great work. This also makes it possible for more children to have their work posted.

The Home-School Connection

A great way to boost the home-school connection is to send a certificate home when a child's work is posted on the star work board. This makes children proud of their work, and it keeps families up to date on their children's progress. (See Appendix K.)

Another way to keep parents and families informed about a child's work is by sending their center folders home for review. I try to send home the center folder once a week. This gives students an ever-greater sense of accountability. To accompany the work, I send home a weekly letter indicating whether the child's center work is satisfactory or unsatisfactory. (See Appendix L for a copy of this letter.)

In the next chapter, I'll show you how I introduce children to the centers in the first weeks of school.

Chapter 5

Getting Started with Centers: The First 8 Weeks

Now that I have shown you how to set up your classroom, how to organize each center, and how to introduce some general routines, let's take a look at how to actually introduce the centers to children at the beginning of the school year. I like to introduce them individually, carefully teaching the procedures and rules for each one. As I mentioned earlier, if you involve children in establishing some of the procedures and rules, they'll be much more likely to follow them—and be more successful learners.

I try to scaffold the learning center experience. First, I model the use of the center. Next, I support students as they begin to use the center by making myself available to answer questions or give guidance when needed. After this modeling and guidance, children are ready to use the centers independently. Getting students to the point where they are completely independent can take between six and eight weeks. But if centers are implemented properly during these first weeks, you will create a wonderful setting for the year to come.

Week I

1. Model how to use the buddy reading center.
2. Use interactive writing to write the rules for buddy reading.

Getting Started

Have a discussion with children about what buddy reading is. Discuss how two children will be reading together and talking about books. Show children where they will get the books that they will be using for buddy reading.

Modeling

Select a student to be your buddy. Choose a book to read together. Model and discuss the many ways that partners can take turns. For instance, each child can read a page or each one can take turns reading every other sentence. Also model the volume at which you want children to read, as well as what careful listening looks like. Be sure to show children how they should put away their buddy reading books.

You may also want to model what it looks like to tell a story through its pictures for your emergent readers. These readers need to know that they can play a part in buddy reading even if they are not sure of all the words. Doing this for these children will help bring their attention to comprehension from the very beginning.

During this first week, I also like to use interactive writing to create the buddy reading rules with my class. In order to keep the interactive writing lessons short and structured, I try to write one rule per day until I have completed the list. Below are some of the rules I have written with my students.

When creating the rules, remember to keep the language simple. Each time the class engages in buddy reading during the first six to eight weeks of school, be sure to read the rules you have written together. This will ensure that they become common knowledge in the classroom. After you have reviewed the rules several times, find a place in your classroom to hang them. This way you can point to the rule to remind children of what to do when they need redirection.

Buddy Reading Rules
1. I will pick a buddy.
2. I will pick a book.
3. I will pick a spot.
4. We will read our books.
5. I will put my book away.

Week 2

1. Review buddy reading rules and practice them daily.
2. Pair up children with mixed abilities.
3. Build up a repertoire of poems.

Continue your work with the buddy reading center, fostering more student independence. Each day, as a class, reread the rules for buddy reading. Then allow children to participate in the buddy reading center for practice. You will need to decide how you want to create your buddy reading partners. I have found it best to partner children with mixed abilities.

You can use the literacy center board (see pages 16–17) to show children who their partners are. I write the partners' names on the center group cards with the buddy reading icon below the names. I write student's names in a way that shows who the pairs are. This helps students become accustomed to using the literacy center board as a tool for knowing what to do during center time.

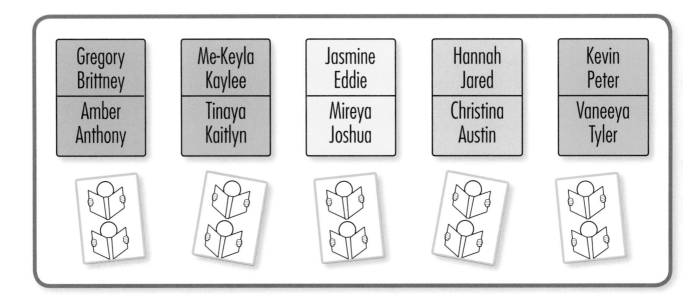

During the first two weeks, I also like to begin creating a repertoire of poems that include many high-frequency words and repetitive language. Having children read these poems helps them develop reading fluency. I type up the poems on individual sheets and store them in the basket. Children know they can choose to read these poems during buddy reading. I like to introduce each poem during shared reading using an enlarged copy of the poem for the whole class to see.

Week 3

1. Introduce the poetry center.
2. Use interactive writing to write the rules for the poetry center.
3. Continue practicing buddy reading.

The next center that I introduce is the poetry center. Each day of the third week, I model one step of this center. We then use interactive writing to write that step. Finally, students participate in the center and complete the step that we had discussed. For instance, the second poetry center step is for students to read a poem to themselves. I model how this should work, and then we use interactive writing to record the step on chart paper. After we've written the step, children read a familiar poem to themselves. I tell children that after they finish at this center, they should move into the buddy reading center. This allows children to move to the next center at their own pace.

Poetry Center Rules
1. I will get my book.
2. I will read my poem.
3. I will cut out my poem.
4. I will glue my poem.
5. I will draw my picture.
6. I will color the picture.

Your work board may look like this during week 3.

Gregory Brittney	Me-Keyla Kaylee	Jasmine Eddie	Hannah Jared	Kevin Peter
Amber Anthony	Tinaya Kaitlyn	Mireya Joshua	Christina Austin	Vaneeya Tyler

Each day, work on a new step of the poetry center, using the same poem.

At the end of center time each day, gather in a circle to discuss how each of the centers went. Share some of the wonderful behaviors you noticed to reinforce appropriate and quality work from your students.

Week 4

1. Practice using the poetry and buddy reading centers.
2. Model use of the listening center.
3. Use interactive writing to write the rules for the listening center.

Continue practicing at both the poetry and the buddy reading centers and begin introducing a third center. I like to introduce the listening center in week four. We complete the steps of the listening center one day at a time as a class. We discuss how to use the tape or CD player and the different roles children can play in pressing the buttons. I model each step, then we write that step on chart paper, and finally we complete the step.

Listening Center Rules
1. I will get a book.
2. We will press play.
3. We will listen to the story.
4. We will press stop.
5. We will work on the paper.
6. We will hand in the paper.

Your work board may look like this during week four.

Gregory Brittney	Me-Keyla Kaylee	Jasmine Eddie	Hannah Jared	Kevin Peter
Amber Anthony	Tinaya Kaitlyn	Mireya Joshua	Christina Austin	Vaneeya Tyler

Week 5

1. Practice using the listening, poetry, and buddy reading centers.

2. Introduce the ABC center.

By week five, your students will have a good understanding of centers. It will be easier for you to start bringing in some new centers and doing others only on certain days. For instance, you may have your class go to the listening center and the poetry center once during the week and the buddy reading center three times, giving you an opportunity to introduce new centers. The next center that I usually introduce is the ABC center. You can implement this center by creating the rules during interactive writing.

Your work board may look like this during week five.

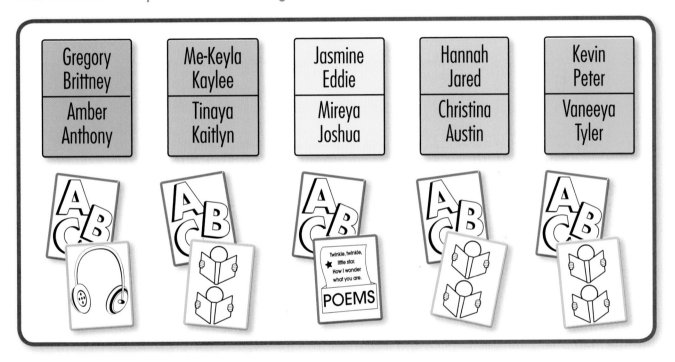

Each day you will need to shift the name cards on your literacy center board one column to the right. The name card at the end will move to the first column on the left. This way, by the end of the week students have rotated through every column on the board.

Week 6

1. Mix around some centers on your work board.
2. Add the writing center.
3. Monitor centers and reinforce rules.

During the sixth week, continue to introduce new centers, such as the writing or handwriting centers. Follow the same steps of modeling, writing the rules, and practicing the center. After students complete each new center, have them rotate through the other centers that they are practicing. While children work at centers, circulate through the room, being sure to visit every student. Take notes on what you notice about how students are working. Reinforce good center behavior as you visit each child.

Your work board may look like this during week six.

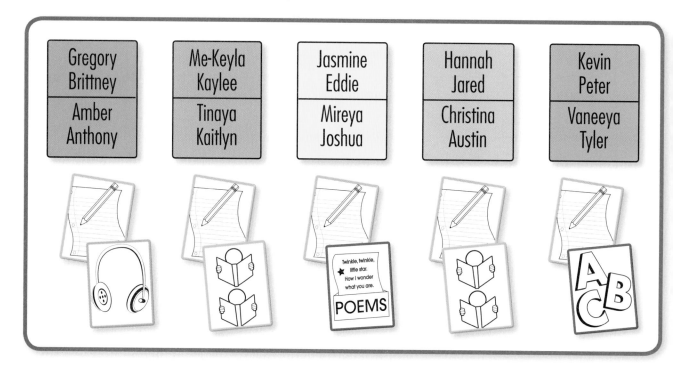

Gregory
Brittney

Amber
Anthony

Me-Keyla
Kaylee

Tinaya
Kaitlyn

Jasmine
Eddie

Mireya
Joshua

Hannah
Jared

Christina
Austin

Kevin
Peter

Vaneeya
Tyler

Twinkle, twinkle, little star. How I wonder what you are.
POEMS

Week 7

W ork toward meeting with one guided reading group per day. Continue to monitor the centers that children are completing during the rest of the time. I also introduce the pocket chart center this week. We work on the rules for this center. Here are the rules my class and I wrote about using a poem in the center.

Pocket Chart Center Rules
1. We will lay out the cards.
2. We will put the cards in order.
3. We will read the poem.
4. We will look for the words.
5. We will put the cards away.

Your work board may look like this during week seven.

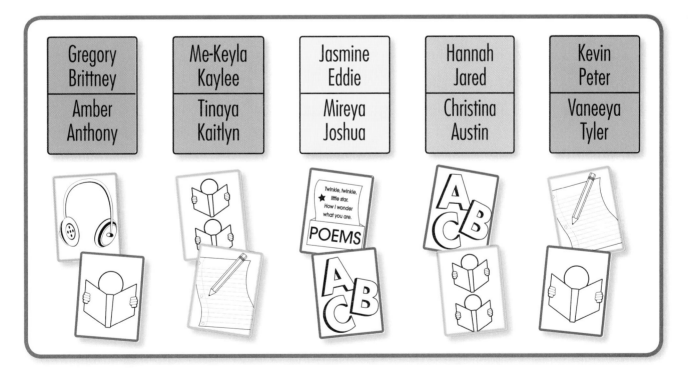

Gregory Brittney	Me-Keyla Kaylee	Jasmine Eddie	Hannah Jared	Kevin Peter
Amber Anthony	Tinaya Kaitlyn	Mireya Joshua	Christina Austin	Vaneeya Tyler

Once your children are working successfully through two centers per day, you can add a third center. Just remember to allow enough time for your students to become independent.

Week 8

1. Work with two guided reading groups per day.

2. Monitor centers in between your groups.

3. Add new centers as needed.

During Week 8

Change the centers on your literacy center board in the way that works best for you in your classroom. I find that some centers work best when visited once a week, while other centers can be visited more than once a week. For instance, I have my children visit the poetry center only one time per week since they work with poetry at other centers as well. Other centers I have my children visit once a week are the listening and the handwriting centers. The rest of the centers provide practice in many word principles and reading strategies, and these centers are visited more than once a week. While your students are at centers this week, try to meet with two reading groups per day. In between meeting with each reading group, walk around the room to monitor the centers while they are in motion. Reinforce students' positive behavior and encourage quality center work during the share time at the end of centers each day to help to keep children on track.

I have put together a composite of what your work board might look like during week eight.

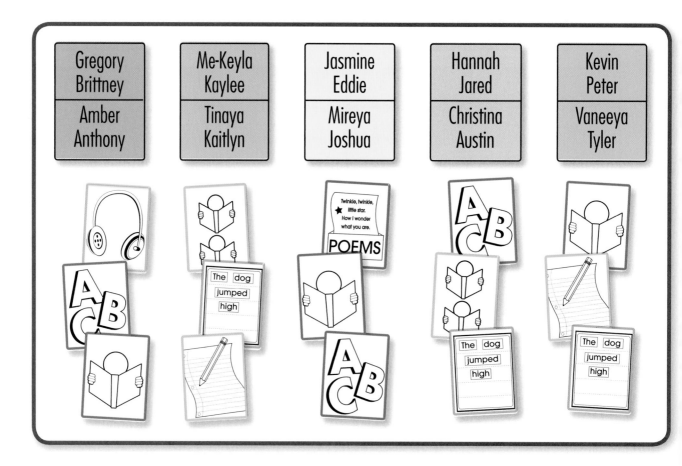

In the next chapter, I'll show you how the centers change after the first eight weeks of school.

Chapter 6

Beyond the
First 8 Weeks

So now your centers are up and running.
What's next? In this chapter, I'll share with you
some of the ways in which I manage center
activities throughout the rest of the year.

Changing Each Center

Center activities should be changed weekly in order to maintain students' interest and to provide consistent practice of new literacy concepts. Each time a center activity is changed, it is important to introduce the new materials or activities so your students can continue to work independently and successfully. Since there are so many different centers going on in the classroom, you may want to think about creating a cycle for changing your centers, rather than introducing all new centers in one day.

One of the ways I accomplish this is by assigning each day a letter. There are A, B, C, D, and E days to represent the five days of the week. Then I decide the order in which to change and introduce new activities. What follows is the schedule I use to change the centers in my classroom.

A	• ABC Center • Poetry Center
B	• Pocket Chart • Handwriting
C	• Art Center • Listening Center
D	• Overhead Center • Writing Center
E	• Magnetic Wall

I find it to be much more manageable to plan a few new centers per day rather than change all the centers at the beginning of each week. It is also easier for students, since they have to take in just a small amount of new information per day.

I use sentence strips to create a schedule for changing my centers. I hang the strips on the wall behind my desk, and I move a clothespin each day to help me keep track of which day I am on. This also makes it easier for students to keep track of which centers have changed.

There are some centers that go hand in hand. For instance, the ABC center, the pocket chart, and the magnetic wall can all involve some kind of word study activity. I like to rotate concepts from one center to the next so that they are practiced for more than just one week. I created a rotation schedule so that I can be sure each concept is practiced in different ways over a three-week period. I also rotate poetry concepts through several centers.

ABC ROTATION
Teach the word study principle in class.
Apply the word study principle at the ABC center.
Apply the word study principle at the magnetic wall center.
Apply the word study principle at the pocket chart center.

POETRY ROTATION
Teach the poem in class during shared reading.
Put the poem at the poetry center.
Put the poem at the pocket chart center.
Put the poem at the overhead center.

Here is an example of how I rotate some word study concepts through my centers.

	Word Study Principle Taught in the Classroom	Word Study Principle Practiced at the ABC Center	Word Study Principle Practiced at the Magnetic Wall Center	Word Study Principle Practiced at the Pocket Chart Center
Week 1	You can change the first letter of a word to make a new word.			
Week 2	You can change the last letter of a word to make a new word.	You can change the first letter of a word to make a new word.		
Week 3	Syllables are word parts. You can count the syllables in a word.	You can change the last letter of a word to make a new word.	You can change the first letter of a word to make a new word.	
Week 4		Syllables are word parts. You can count the syllables in a word.	You can change the last letter of a word to make a new word.	You can change the first letter of a word to make a new word.
Week 5			Syllables are word parts. You can count the syllables in a word.	You can change the last letter of a word to make a new word.

Appendices

This section includes the icons, letters, and response sheets that I use at my centers. You can reproduce these pages as needed. You may want to copy, color, and laminate the guided reading calling cards. You may also want to color and laminate the icons when you use them for the literacy center board.

The star work icons on pages 93 and 95 are designed to be cut out for you to use on your bulletin board. Again, you may want to laminate them to make them sturdier.

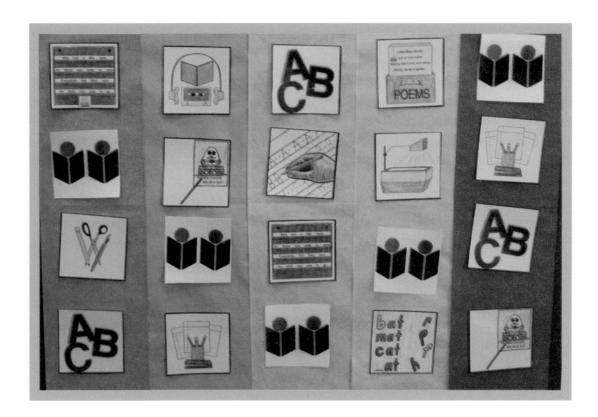

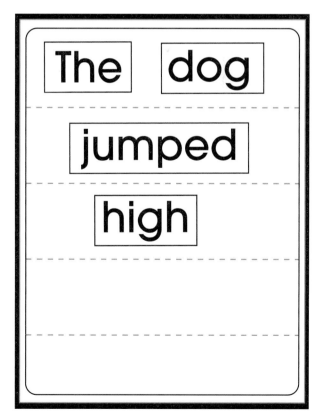

Twinkle, twinkle,
little star.
How I wonder
what you are.

POEMS

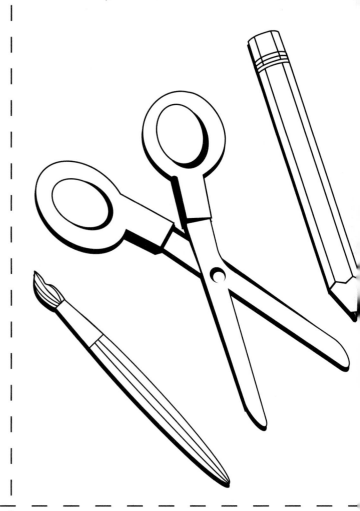

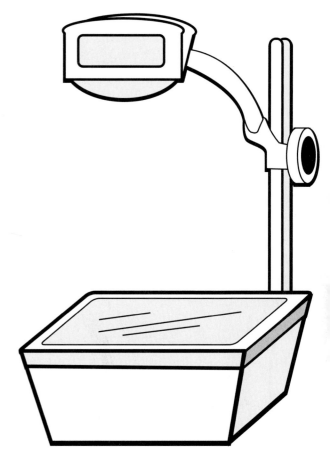

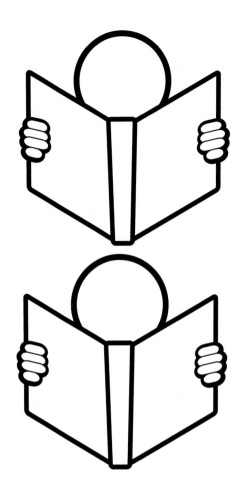

Dear Parent(s)/Guardian(s),

Welcome to _____ grade! Throughout the year, we will be completing many projects and assignments that require a great deal of supplies. I have created a list of supplies that each child is responsible for having in the classroom. Please have your child bring in the following supplies to school on the first day or as soon as possible after school begins:

❏ 12 #2 pencils

❏ 1 4-count package of dry-erase markers

❏ 1 smock for art

❏ 1 48-count box of crayons

❏ 1 package of thin markers

❏ 1 package of thick markers

❏ 1 package of baby wipes

❏ 1 blunt-tip scissors

❏ 3 black-and-white marble notebooks

❏ 5 large glue sticks

❏ 2 boxes of tissues

These supplies will be shared among the children in the classroom in order to build a sharing and caring community, so please don't label anything with your child's name. Please keep in mind that I may request other materials for special projects during the year. If you have any problems finding any of these materials or any questions regarding this list, please contact me during the first week of school.

Thank you so much for helping your child be successful in our classroom. I look forward to meeting you soon!

Sincerely,

_____

Dear Parent(s)/Guardian(s),

Your children and I are going to start off the year by getting to know one another through storytelling. To help children think of stories to tell, it is helpful for them to have reminders. Your child is being asked to create a storytelling bag. Please follow the instructions below to create the storytelling bag and aid your child in the journey of storytelling.

1. Find a large, sturdy zip-lock bag.

2. Fill the bag with items to represent memories! Try to find at least eight items to put into the storytelling bag.

Here are some examples of items that will prompt stories:

❏ A baseball might remind a child of a story about playing or attending a baseball game.

❏ A picture of a pet might call to mind a story that your child would like to tell about that pet.

❏ A trinket from a vacation might spark a memory that your child would like to share with the class about the vacation.

The possibilities are endless!

3. Remember, whatever your child brings must fit in the storytelling bag! Any items that are too large will be sent back home.

Bring the storytelling bag to school by: _____

I can't wait to hear the many stories your child has to tell!

Thank you,

_____

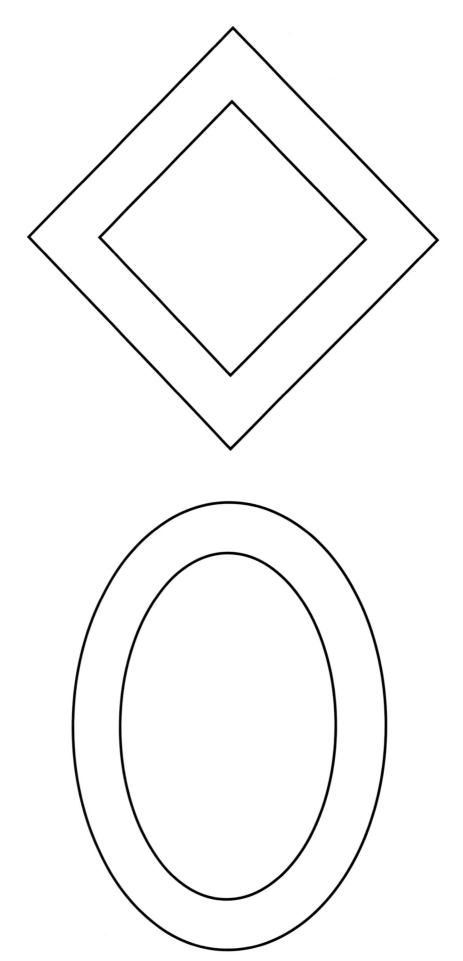

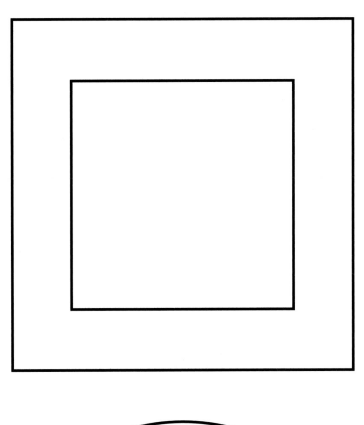

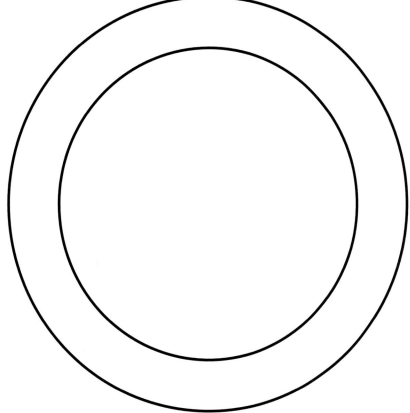

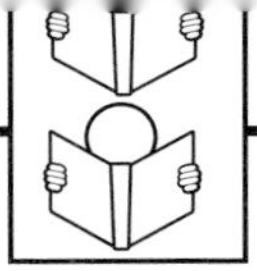

Buddy Reading Record Sheet

Date _____

Buddy _____

Title _____

Author _____

Date _____

Buddy _____

Title _____

Author _____

Independent Reading Record Sheet

Date

Title

Author

Date

Title

Author

Listening Center Response Sheet (early)

Name: _____   Date: _____

Title: _____

_____

Author: _____

Circle One

 I loved the story | I liked the story | I did not like the story

Draw a picture of your favorite part of the story.

Listening Center Response Sheet (written)

Name: _____ Date: _____

Title: _____

_____

Author: _____

_____

Response: -

_____

_____

- -

_____

_____

- -

_____

_____

- -

_____

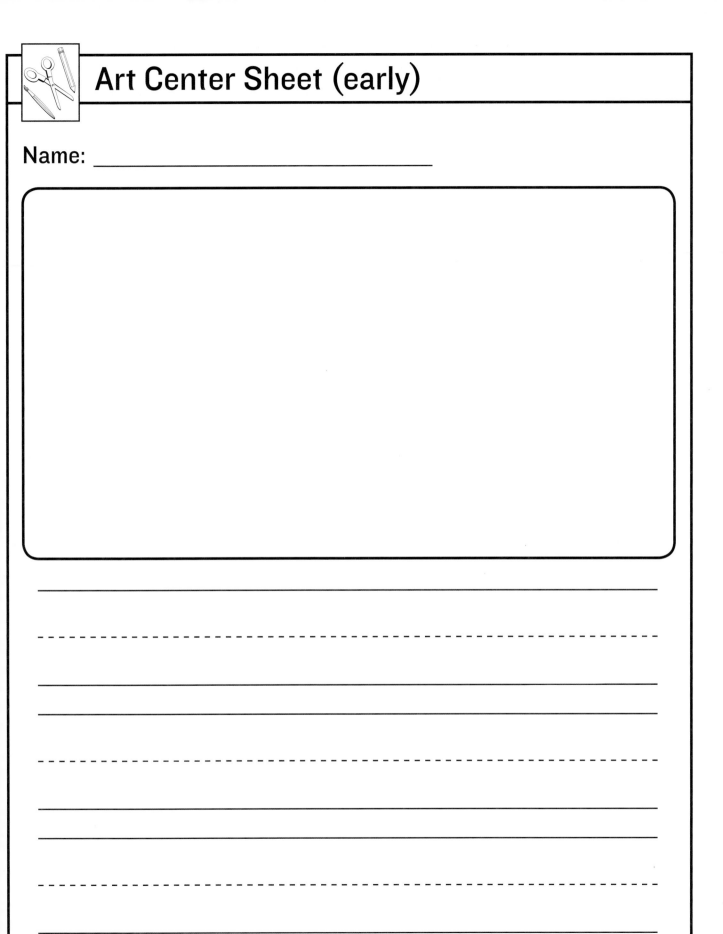

Art Center Sheet (early)

Name: _____

Art Center Sheet (written)

Name: _____ **Date:** _____

_____

Response: -

_____

_____

- -

_____

- -

_____

- -

_____

- -

_____

- -

_____

- -

_____

- -

Great Job!

has completed his / her center work with exceptional quality.

This work will be posted in the classroom as an example of fantastic work!

Week of _____

Dear Parent(s)/Guardian(s),

In our classroom, your child has been working at various centers. This work is completed independently, without any teacher support. The center activities reinforce lessons we have learned in the classroom. Attached to this page you will find a folder with the work your child has finished during center time this week. I have made some comments on your child's work that I would like you to review with him or her at home. Once you have reviewed the work, please sign the work at the bottom and return the folder (with the work inside it) to school on Monday. It is very important to return the folder to school because we use these folders on a daily basis. At the end of the year, all of your child's center work will be sent home for you to keep. Enjoy your weekend!

Thank you,

_____

Your child's center work this week was:

❏ SATISFACTORY   ❏ UNSATISFACTORY

Teacher Comments (if necessary): _____

_____

Parent Signature: _____ Date: _____

Parent Comments: _____

_____

_____

The dog jumped high

Twinkle, twinkle, little star. How I wonder what you are.

POEMS

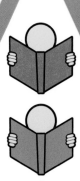